A Beginner's Guide TO Interpreting Bible Prophecy

A 5-PART STUDY

A Beginner's Guide TO Interpreting Bible Prophecy

Introduction

For many Christians, interpreting Bible prophecy is a complicated task. As a result, they often turn to so-called Bible experts and complicated charts that include gaps in time, outrageous literal interpretations, and numerous claims that current events are prime indicators that the end is near. Many Christians are unaware that the same Bible passages have been used in nearly every generation as "proof" that the end or some aspect of the end (the "rapture") would take place in their generation.

They've all had one thing in common: They've all been wrong.

With so much prophetic material in the Bible – somewhere around 25% of the total makeup of Scripture – it seems difficult to argue that an expert is needed to understand such a large portion of God's Word and so many "experts" could be wrong generation after generation. If God's Word is a lamp to our feet and a light to our path" (Psalm 119:105), how do we explain that not a lot of light has been shed on God's prophetic Word with so little accuracy?

A Beginner's Guide to Interpreting Bible Prophecy is an attempt to remedy the confusion over what the Bible says about prophetic material. It begins with the operating premise that the Bible is the best interpreter of itself.

For nearly 2000 years Christians have attempted to read and interpret Scripture through the lens of current events without paying close attention to audience relevance, specific time indicators, the literal translation and comparison of specific words found in prophetic texts, and the transition between the Old and New Testaments.

A Beginner's Guide to Interpreting Bible Prophecy

The Bible can be an intimidating book. It does not have to be. It's my prayer that this short guide to Bible prophecy will help you to be like the Bereans who examined "the Scriptures daily *to see* whether these things were so" (Acts 17:11).

Paul Preaching to the Bereans

A Beginner's Guide TO Interpreting Bible Prophecy

PART 1

What is Prophecy?

Predictive prophecy (foretelling) is about the future. This type of Bible prophecy is about what God says is going to happen in the future.

There is also a type of prophecy that is called *forthtelling*, applying God's word to every aspect of life. This type of prophecy may or may not have predictive elements as part of the exhortation.

There are many Bible-based prophecies that have already been fulfilled. Their fulfillment is in our past. This shows that God's Word is true and can be trusted. Predictive prophecy of this type must be 100% accurate (Deut. 18:22).

> Prophecy, when spelled with a "**c**," is a noun. "Revelation is a book about prophe**c**y."
>
> Prophesy, spelled with an "**s**," is a verb. "A prophet is given a gift by God to prophe**s**y about what will happen in the future."

Many prophecies found in the Old Testament refer to the coming of a promised Savior, Jesus Christ.

- **Place of birth: Bethlehem** (Micah 5:2; Matt. 2:5–6; Luke 2:4)

- **Time of birth: based on the seventy weeks of years given to Daniel** (Dan. 9:25; Luke 2:25–32)

- **Manner of birth: born of a virgin** (Is. 7:14; Luke 1:34)

- **Price of betrayal: thirty pieces of silver** (Zech. 11:12; Matt. 26:15; 27:9–10)

- **Manner of death: crucifixion** (Ps. 22:16, 18; Matt. 27:35; Luke 23:34; John 19:24; 20:25)

- **Condition of the body: no broken bones** (Ps. 34:20; John 19:31–33)

- but a pierced side (Zech. 12:10; John 19:34, 37)

- **Loyalty of his disciples: deserted by His followers** (Zech. 13:7; Matt. 26:31)

- **Burial place: buried in a rich man's tomb** (Is. 53:9; Matt. 27:57–30)

The chance that any one person could have fulfilled all eight prophecies is 1 chance in 100,000,000,000,000,000 or 1 in 100 quadrillion. Jesus had no control over the fulfillment of these prophecies. For example, He could not choose where He was born, how He would die, where He would be buried, or that no one would break His legs.

One man has calculated that there are more than 330 distinct predictions that Jesus fulfilled.[1] The chance that any one person fulfilled just 48 prophecies is 1 in 10^{157}. This number is so large—1 followed by 157 zeros—as to be unimaginable.[2]

Other prophecies in the Bible tell what will happen to people, cities, and nations.

For example, the Bible predicts in Ezekiel 26:4–5 that the walls and towers of Tyre will be destroyed and her debris will be scraped from her so she will be a "bare rock" where fishermen will spread their nets. Many nations did come against Tyre, and in 332 BC, Alexander the Great and his troops literally scraped the rubble from the mainland and used it to build a causeway so he could lead his forces to attack the island fortress.[3]

The Old Testament predicts what would happen to Assyria, Babylon, Persia, Greece, Rome, and Israel in the years leading up to the entry of Jesus into the world.

Like the Old Testament, the New Testament is filled with prophetic material. Some people believe that most of these prophecies are yet to be fulfilled. Others believe they have already been fulfilled. How do we know who is right?

Scripture Interprets Scripture

The first place to start in learning how to interpret **prophecy** is to learn how to interpret the Bible, because the Bible is the best interpreter of itself. This statement seems so obvious, and yet many people fail to follow it. When the subject of prophecy comes up, some eager prophecy students read the Bible through the headlines of the newspaper. When news stories report about earthquakes, wars and rumors of wars, and famines, these are immediately seen by many as "signs" that prophecy is being fulfilled right before our eyes.

There have been earthquakes, wars and rumors of wars, and famines for thousands of years. Why are they signs **now** when they were thought to be signs 60 years ago, 100 years ago, and 250 years ago for people living then? In fact, for nearly 2000 years there have always been people who claimed that the end was near for them. How could they be wrong about something the Bible talks a lot about? Can the Bible be that hard to understand?

Time Keys

When signs are given, there are often **time keys** present to inform the reader when to look for the signs. For example, Jesus said that after He was killed, He would "be raised up on the third day" (Matt. 16:21). "Third day" is a time key. There are less specific time keys like "soon," "near," "shortly," "quickly," and "at hand." We'll look at these time keys in a moment.

Sometimes there are time keys that require comparing Scripture with Scripture. For example, Jesus said, "**This generation** will not pass away until all these things take place" (Matt. 24:34). Some of "all these things" are earthquakes, wars, and famines. They were to take place before "this generation" passed away. If we can figure out what "this generation" means, then we will know something about when to look for these signs.

Jesus is the Bible's best teacher, so let's begin with what He has to say about this important subject. When Jesus' disciples heard Him tell the religious leaders that the temple was going to be destroyed (Matt. 23:38), they asked Him when this would happen. While He was sitting on the Mount of Olives just outside of Jerusalem, He explained to them what was going to take place in the near future — their future (Matt. 24; Mark 13; Luke 21).

In fact, they would be the ones to see these signs (Matt. 24:33).

This step-by-step prophecy is filled with details about what was going to happen to the temple that was standing in Jesus' day (Matt. 24:1-2), in Judea (24:16), Jerusalem (23:37), the **end of the age** (*aion*) not the end of the "world" (*kosmos*) as some translations have it, (24:3), and **their generation** (24:34). Jesus told His disciples that *they* would see certain things take place before *their* generation passed away (Matt. 23:36; 24:34).

The key to knowing when the Olivet Discourse was or will be fulfilled is by knowing what Jesus meant by "this generation."

> Matthew 24:3 is more accurately translated as "**the end of the age**" (a period of time) rather than "the end of the world" (planet earth).

Since we know the Bible interprets the Bible, we can determine what Jesus meant by finding other places where "this generation" is used. Jesus uses "this generation" in several places in Matthew, Mark, and Luke. Each time "this generation" is used it means the people who were living at that time. Don't take my word for it. Check out the verses for yourself. "**This generation**" is never used by Jesus to refer to a future generation.

If Jesus had a future generation in mind, He could have said "*that* generation." When "this" is used in the Bible, this refers to something that is near, while "that" most often refers to some event in the future: "Many will say to Me on *that* day, 'Lord, Lord, did we not prophesy in Your name, and in Your name cast out demons, and in Your name perform many miracles?'" (Matt. 7:22).

Some interpreters argue that it's "this *kind* of *evil* generation." Of course, Jesus does not say "this kind of evil generation will not pass away until all these things take place." In order to get this meaning, words have to be added to the text.

For a long time, some interpreters claimed that Jesus meant "this *race* will not pass away until all these things take place. There are several problems with translating the Greek word *genea* as "race." First, it's the wrong Greek word. If Jesus wanted to say "race," He would have used *genos*.

Second, translating *genea* as "race" makes no logical sense since when all these things take place the Jewish race will pass away. Jesus is referring to a period of time and the people who are living during that period of time, not a "race" of people.

Third, the places where *genea* is used the word "race" does not fit the context. For example, try replacing "generation" in Matthew 1:17 with "race": "So all the *races* from Abraham to David are fourteen *races*; from David to the deportation to Babylon, fourteen *races*; and from the deportation to Babylon to the Messiah, fourteen *races*."

"This Generation"
- Matthew 11:16
- Matthew 12:41
- Matthew 12:42
- Matthew 23:36
- Mark 8:12
- Luke 7:31
- Luke 11:31
- Luke 11:32
- Luke 11:50
- Luke 11:51
- Luke 17:52

Fourth, nearly every commentator interprets Matthew 23:36 as referring to the generation to whom Jesus was speaking. Why would Jesus change the meaning of "this generation" when speaking to His disciples who heard Him use the same phrase when He was speaking to "the multitude" and them (23:1). As Jesus does in chapter 24, He uses the second person plural "you" in chapter 23 (vv. 13, 16, 23, 27, 29, 31, 33–36).

Notes

1. Floyd E. Hamilton, *The Basis of Christian Faith: A Modern Defense of the Christian Religion*, rev. ed. (New York: Harper & Row, 1964), 160.

2. Peter W. Stoner, *Science Speaks: Scientific Proof of the Accuracy of Prophecy and the Bible*, 3rd rev. ed. (Chicago, IL: Moody Press, 1969), 109.

3. J. P. Holding, "Steel-Belted Tyre: On the Tyre Prophecy of Ezekiel www.tektonics.org/uz/zeketyre.html; Trevor Major, "The Fall of Tyre" (December 1996): www.apologeticspress.org/articles/254; John A. Bloom," Is Fulfilled Prophecy of Value for Scholarly Apologetics?" (November 1995): www.trinitysem.edu/journal/prophesy.html

A Beginner's Guide
TO Interpreting Bible Prophecy

PART 2

Identify the Primary Audience

In addition to paying close attention to when prophetic events are said to take place, it's important to identify the *primary audience*, the audience that will see the events unfold. How would the original audience have understood what Jesus was saying? When you read the Olivet Discourse in Matthew 24, Mark 13, and Luke 21, you should notice that Jesus uses the second person plural "you" many times throughout the passage.

- "Do *you* not see all these things" (Matt. 24:2).

- "And Jesus answered and said to them, 'See to it that no one misleads *you*'" (24:4).

- "You will be hearing of wars and rumors of wars. See that *you* are not frightened, for those things must take place, but that is not yet the end" (24:6).

- "Then they will deliver *you* to tribulation, and will kill *you*, and *you* will be hated by all nations because of My name" (24:9).

Jesus is obviously addressing the disciples who pointed out the temple buildings to Him. They were the ones who would see "all these things."

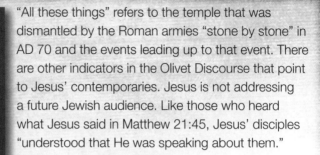

"All these things" refers to the temple that was dismantled by the Roman armies "stone by stone" in AD 70 and the events leading up to that event. There are other indicators in the Olivet Discourse that point to Jesus' contemporaries. Jesus is not addressing a future Jewish audience. Like those who heard what Jesus said in Matthew 21:45, Jesus' disciples "understood that He was speaking about them."

There are those who argue for a generic meaning for "you." There are many occasions in the Bible, the argument goes, in which God speaks to an immediate, physically present audience, but actually a future group of individuals is the audience the Bible has in mind. There are times when this may be true.

But as we see in Matthew 24:2, the use of "you" is obviously a reference to the disciples who asked the question about the temple. Jesus is answering them and includes them and their generation in the prophetic events as they transpire. Since "all these things" (Matt. 24:33) take place within the time context of "this generation" (Matt. 23:36; 24:34; Mark 13:30; Luke 21:32), there is no need to project these prophetic events into an unspecified future.

It's the same audience that Jesus warns not to be misled: "See to it that no one misleads you (24:4). The audience doesn't change when Jesus says, "*you* will be hearing of wars and rumors of wars" (24:6).

Jesus warns this same group of disciples that their enemies "will deliver *you* up to tribulation" (24:9). We certainly know this happened by reading the book of Acts and Paul's letters (e.g., Acts 7:54–60; 14:19; 2 Cor. 11:22–27). Jesus tells them to "pray that *your*

BC and AD

When you see a date that is followed by **BC**, it's telling you the event took place or the person lived that many years "Before Christ" was born. **AD** refers to events that took place or when a person lived since Jesus was born. **AD** is an abbreviation for *anno domini*, a Latin phrase that means "in the year of our Lord."

flight will not be in the winter or on a Sabbath" (Matt. 24:20). Before Jesus says "this generation will not pass away until all these things take place," He confirms everything He told them would take place with these words: *"So, you too, when you see all these things, recognize that He is near, right at the door"* (24:33). "You" means **them**, not us. Those who saw "all these things" in verse 3 are the same ones who see "all these things" in verse 33.

If Jesus had wanted to warn a future generation, He would have said "when *they* see" and *"they* will be hearing of wars and rumors of wars." The use of "you" and not "they" throughout the chapter explains why the Olivet Discourse is not about a future generation.

There are some additional audience hints that can tell us when the events outlined by Jesus in Matthew 24 took place. The tribulation was a local event. It could be escaped by fleeing on foot "to the mountains" surrounding Jerusalem (Matt 24:16). If Jesus had been describing a global event, there would be no place to escape or hide, and foot travel would be impractical and futile. The people are living in houses that have flat roofs (24:17), the economy is mostly agricultural (24:18), and the Sabbath is still observed (24:20). These geographical clues indicate that Jesus is describing first-century Judea, not the whole wide world.

What Does the Passage Say?

Many people grow up thinking the Bible says one thing when it actually says something else. For example, when asked who cut off Samson's hair, a high percentage of people will say "Delilah!" By

The prophet "Agabus stood up and began to indicate by the Spirit that there would certainly be a great famine all over the world. And this took place in the reign of Claudius" (Acts 11:28).

As we will see the greek word "world" in this passage is not the usual word for "world."

reading Judges 16:19, we quickly learn that she "called for a man and had him shave off the seven locks of his hair." If you were to ask someone who is familiar with the Bible what animal will lie down with the lamb, most likely he or she will say "the lion." Isaiah 11:6 says that it's the wolf that will dwell with the lamb (also see 65:25).

Before we can know what a passage *means*, we must first determine what it *says*. We are not permitted to add words and ideas to the Bible that aren't there (Rev. 22:18–19). Here's what one prophecy writer claims: "Jesus said the last generation would witness unprecedented increases in earthquakes, famines, wars and pestilences."[1]

First, nothing is said about a "last generation." Jesus says "this generation." If we take the view that "you" does not mean them, and "this" does not refer to their generation, then how would Jesus have said it if He meant them and their generation if "you" does not mean them and "this generation" does not mean their generation?

Second, this is what Jesus actually told His first-century audience: "Nation

Jesus Predicts the Destruction of Jerusalem

will rise against nation and kingdom against kingdom, and there will be great[2] earthquakes, and in various places plagues and famines; and there will be terrors and great signs from heaven" (Luke 21:11). There is no mention of the number, magnitude, or increase of earthquakes. He only states that there will be "great earthquakes" before that first-century generation passes away. Records of earthquakes go back thousands of years (e.g., Amos 1:1; Zech. 14:5), and they were a part of Israel's history in the first century leading up to the destruction of Jerusalem in AD 70. Even great earthquakes![3]

The New Testament records three earthquakes that took place in the days of the apostles, two of which are said to have been "great" (Matt. 27:54; 28:2; Acts 16:26). Tacitus, a historian who lived in the first century, mentions earthquakes that were so great that "immense mountains sank down . . . level places were seen to be elevated into hills, and . . . fires flashed forth during the catastrophe."[4]

In AD 61, just nine years before the destruction of the temple and the

Tacitus (c. AD 56–c. 117) mentions earthquakes that were so great that "immense mountains sank down . . . level places were seen to be elevated into hills."

fall of Jerusalem in AD 70, an earthquake struck the city of Laodicea in Asia Minor. Here's how Tacitus described it: "Laodicea was destroyed by an earthquake . . . and rebuilt from its resources without any [help] from Rome."[5]

Like earthquakes, famines were also common in the first century (Luke 15:14; Rom. 8:35; 1 Cor. 16:1–3). There was a "great famine" throughout the Roman Empire (Acts 11:28) during the time Claudius Caesar ruled.

There was a "great famine" throughout the Roman Empire (Acts 11:28) during the reign of Claudius Caesar.

Notes

1. Hal Lindsey, "Gloom and doom, prophecy and hope" (October 26, 2007): www.worldnetdaily.com/news/article.asp?ARTICLE_ID=58356

2. Only Luke uses the word "great" in his description of the earthquakes (see Matt. 24:7 and Mark 13:8).

3. George Adam Smith, *Jerusalem: The Topography, Economics and History from the Earliest Times to AD 70* (London: Hodder and Stoughton, 1907), 61–74.

4. Description of earthquakes in the first century by the historian Tacitus (c. AD 56–117) in his historical work *The Annals* (2.47): www.chieftainsys.freeserve.co.uk/tacitus_annals02.htm

5. Tacitus, *The Annals* (14.27): www.chieftainsys.freeserve.co.uk/tacitus_annals14.htm

A Beginner's Guide TO Interpreting Bible Prophecy

PART 3

Knowing Some Greek Can Help

The New Testament is written in Greek. Since most of us don't know how to read Greek, we are left to trust the translations we use. Some translations are better than others. Translations that work to produce the most literal translation are the best even if they do not always read smoothly. Unfortunately, faithfulness to the text in translation is not always followed. For example, in Matthew 24:14, most English translations have the passage read like this:

> "This gospel of the kingdom shall be preached in the **whole world** as a testimony to all the nations, and then the end will come."

The translation "whole world" might lead a student of the Bible to expect that the gospel must be preached to every person around the globe before the end of the age takes place. This interpretation, unfortunately, is based on a bad translation.

There are three Greek words in the New Testament that are sometimes translated "world": αιων (aion), κοσμος (kosmos), and οικουμενη (oikoumenē). While you may not be able to read Greek, you can see that

Greek Alphabet

A, α (alpha) = a
B, β (beta) = b
Γ, γ (gamma) = g
Δ, δ (delta) = d
E, ε (epsilon) = e
Z, ζ (zeta) = z
H η (eta) = e
Θ, θ (theta) = th
I, ι (iota) = i
K, κ (kappa) = k
Λ, λ (lambda) = l
M, μ (mu) = m
N, ν (nu) = n
Ξ, ξ (xi) = x
O, o (omicron) = o
Π, π (pi) = p
P, ρ (rho) = r
Σ, σ, ς (sigma)[1] = s
T, τ (tau) = t
Y, υ (upsilon) = u
Φ, φ (phi) = ph
X, χ (chi) = ch
Ψ, ψ (psi) = ps
Ω, ω (omega) = o

[1]σ is used inside a word while ς is used at the end of a word (κοσμος). They are both pronounced "s."

As in English, there are blends in Greek: αι = ai (rain) and οι = oi (oil)

the words look different when compared to one another. More importantly, they have different meanings. The Greek word αιων, as we have already noted, means "age," a period of time (1 Cor. 10:11).

Κοσμος is a familiar word since the English words "cosmic" (pertaining to the universe), "cosmology" (study or nature of the universe), and "cosmopolitan" (having worldwide scope) are derived from it.

When the Bible tells us, "For God so loved the **world**" (John 3:16), the Greek word κοσμος is used and refers to Jews, Samaritans, and Gentiles — the world as we usually understand the word (4:39–42). Like in English, however, the Bible's use of "world" (κοσμος) can refer to something less than the entire globe (e.g., Rom. 1:8).

Jesus does not use αιων or κοσμος in Matthew 24:14. The word He chooses to make His point about how far the gospel will be preached before that first generation passes is οικουμενη, the "inhabited earth" or "the known world" of the day. We can get some idea of the meaning of οικουμενη by looking at other places where the word is used.

In Luke 2:1 we read, as some translations have it, "Now it came about in those days that a decree went out from Caesar Augustus that a census be taken of all the **world**" (Luke 2:1). It's highly unlikely that Caesar took a census of people living in China, India, and North and South America.

Luke uses οικουμενη and not κοσμος, so we don't have to guess what he means about the geographical extent of the taxing powers of the

Roman Empire. Because οικουμενη is used, Luke 2:1 should read like this: "Now in those days a decree went out from Caesar Augustus, that a census be taken of all **the inhabited earth**" (or the "known world" or "Roman Empire" since the tax is Roman).

Remember the famine that Luke described in Acts 11:28 as being "all over the world"? Well, the Greek word translated "world" is οικουμενη, "the inhabited earth." This means that the famine was most likely limited to the Roman Empire.

How does this short study help in our understanding of Matthew 24:14? If the census and the famine covered an area limited to the Roman Empire, then it's most likely that the same is true for the extent of the gospel proclamation.

Was the gospel preached throughout the "inhabited earth," the known world of the first-century, before the Roman armies invaded and destroyed the temple in Jerusalem in AD 70? What does the Bible say?

Let's compare Scripture with Scripture. Paul writes that the faith of the Romans was "being proclaimed throughout the **whole world**" (Rom. 1:8). In this case, the Greek word *kosmos* is used. So even if Jesus had used *kosmos* in Matthew 24:14, the passage in Romans 1:8 could be used to show that the passage was fulfilled in Paul's day.

Paul tells the Colossians that the gospel had come to them and "was constantly bearing fruit and increasing" in "**all the world**" (Col. 1:6). Again,

Οικουμενη
(oikoumenē)
"Inhabited Earth"

- Now it came about in those days that a decree went out from Caesar Augustus, that a census be taken of all the inhabited earth" (Luke 2:1).

- "And one of [the prophets] named Agabus stood up and began to indicate by the Spirit that there would certainly be a great famine over all the inhabited earth. And this took place in the reign of Claudius" (Acts 11:28).

- "And this gospel of the kingdom shall be preached in all the inhabited earth for a witness to all the nations, and then the end shall come" (Matt. 24:14).

kosmos is used. The gospel had advanced so far throughout the Roman Empire that Paul could say that it "was proclaimed in **all creation under heaven**" (1:23).

All the Nations

By knowing some Greek, your understanding of what the Bible says can help in interpreting what it means. In the case of Matthew 24:14, the gospel had been preached as far as Jesus said it would be preached before the temple was destroyed (24:2), before that first-century generation passed away (24:34). How do we know this? Because Jesus said it would happen that way, and the Bible confirms it.

Not only does Matthew 24:14 say that the "gospel of the kingdom shall be preached in the whole inhabited earth," but it also says that such preaching would be "a testimony to all the nations."

This language is similar to what we read early in the book of Acts: "Now there were Jews living in Jerusalem, devout men, from **every nation under heaven**" (Acts 2:6). Paul writes to Timothy that the gospel was "proclaimed **among the nations**" and "believed on in the world" (1 Tim. 3:16). In the letter to the Romans, Paul writes in the concluding chapter:

Paul wrote that the gospel had been "proclaimed among the nations"
(1 Tim. 3:16) to "all creation under heaven" (Col. 1:23).

Now to Him who is able to establish you according
to my gospel and the preaching of Jesus Christ,
according to the revelation of the mystery which
has been kept secret for long ages past, but now is
manifested, and by the Scriptures of the prophets,
according to the commandment of the eternal God,
has been made known to all the nations, leading to
obedience of faith; to the only wise God, through Jesus
Christ, be the glory forever. Amen. (Rom. 16:25-27)

Help from Hebrew and Greek Interlinear Bibles

One of the most useful tools in helping the novice language student see what
words are being translated into English is the use of an *interlinear* where each
Hebrew and Greek word is shown with its English translation (most often
translated literally) and linked to a Hebrew and Greek dictionary.

There are print and free online editions available.

Zondervan publishes John R. Kohlenberger's *Interlinear NIV Hebrew-English
Old Testament*. Hebrew is more difficult to learn. For the beginner, Greek is
the place to start.

There are many print format Greek-English interlinear New Testaments
available. The one I find most helpful is Paul R. McReynolds' *Word Study
Greek-English New Testament* that includes a dictionary based on James
Strong's numbering system that is found in *Strong's Exhaustive Bible
Concordance.*

Each original-language word [in *Strong's Exhaustive
Bible Concordance*] is given an entry number in
the dictionary of those original language words
listed in the back of the concordance. These have
become known as the "Strong's numbers." The main
concordance lists each word that appears in the KJV
Bible in alphabetical order with each verse in which

Titus removing the vessels from the temple in AD 70

it appears listed in order of its appearance in the
Bible, with a snippet of the surrounding text (including
the word in italics). Appearing to the right of [the]
Scripture reference is the Strong's number. This allows
the user of the concordance to look up the meaning
of the original language word in the associated
dictionary in the back, thereby showing how the
original language word was translated into the English
word in the KJV Bible."

If you are looking for online versions of Hebrew and Greek interlinear Bibles,
there are numerous sites that include them free of charge. The following is
from Biblehub.com. Here's what a Greek interlinear apparatus looks like on
Matthew 24:14:

◄ Matthew 24:14 ►

Matthew 24 Interlinear

	2532 [e]	2784 [e]		3778 [e]	3588 [e]	2098 [e]		3588 [e]	932 [e]		1722 [e]	3650 [e]	3588 [e]	3625 [e]
	kai	kērychthēsetai		touto	to	euangelion		tēs	basileias		en	holē	tē	oikoumenē
14	καὶ	κηρυχθήσεται		τοῦτο	τὸ	εὐαγγέλιον		τῆς	βασιλείας		ἐν	ὅλῃ	τῇ	οἰκουμένῃ ,
	And	there will be proclaimed		this	-	gospel		of the	kingdom		in	all	the	earth
	Conj	V-FIP-3S		DPro-NNS	Art-NNS	N-NNS		Art-GFS	N-GFS		Prep	Adj-DFS	Art-DFS	N-DFS

1519 [e]	3142 [e]	3956 [e]	3588 [e]	1484 [e]		2532 [e]	5119 [e]	2240 [e]	3588 [e]	5056 [e]
eis	martyrion	pasin	tois	ethnesin		kai	tote	hēxei	to	telos
εἰς	μαρτύριον	πᾶσιν	τοῖς	ἔθνεσιν ;		καὶ	τότε	ἥξει	τὸ	τέλος .
for	a testimony	to all	the	nations		and	then	will come	the	end
Prep	N-ANS	Adj-DNP	Art-DNP	N-DNP		Conj	Adv	V-FIA-3S	Art-NNS	N-NNS

Οἰκουμένη: It includes Strong's numbering system (3625: "inhabited earth"),
an English transliteration (*oikoumenē*), the Greek word used (οἰκουμένη),
and lexicographical information (noun, dative, feminine, singular) for more
advanced students. Once you learn the Greek alphabet, and get comfortable
with pronunciation, it's easy to compare one passage with another where the
same Hebrew or Greek words are used and their English translations.

A Beginner's Guide TO Interpreting Bible Prophecy

PART 4

What Does it Mean to Interpret the Bible Literally?

Some time ago I received the following email from a concerned Bible student:

> Please read the following passage and tell me how the statement could possibly be true if the writers of the Bible knew the Earth was round: "The tree grew, and was strong, and the height thereof reached unto heaven, and the sight thereof to the end of all the Earth" (Dan. 4:11) The Bible also clearly says the Sun rotates around the Earth: "Also, the sun rises and the sun sets; and hastening to its place it rises there *again*" (Eccl. 1:5). If the Bible is the true Word of God, then God believes the Sun rotates around a flat Earth.

Most new Christians are told to interpret the Bible literally, but they are almost never told what "literal" actually means or how the principle can be applied consistently without damaging the integrity of the Bible. Here's a popular definition of what constitutes a "literal interpretation of the Bible":

> The best guide to Bible study is "The Golden Rule of Biblical Interpretation." To depart from this rule opens

the student to all forms of confusion and sometimes even heresy. When the plain sense of Scripture makes common sense, seek no other sense, but take every word at its primary, literal meaning unless the facts of the immediate context clearly indicate otherwise.[1]

Eretz

The Hebrew word *eretz* can be translated as "earth" or "land" (Ex. 10:12–15) depending on the context, especially when the "land of Israel" is the context. The same is true for the Greek word *ge*, from which we get the word *ge*ography, "from the Greek word γεωγραφία (*geographia*), lit. 'earth description'": "Get up, take the Child and His mother, and go into the land (*gē*) of Israel; for those who sought the Child's life are dead" (Matt. 2:20; also 4:15; 9:31; 10:15). Translating *gē* as "earth" would not make sense.

If we follow this so-called Golden Rule of interpretation, then the man with the questions about a flat and stationary earth is correct. The Bible teaches that the earth is flat, is positioned at the center of the solar system, does not move (Psalm 93:1), and rests on pillars. In reality, the Bible is not describing the shape of the earth, its physical position in the cosmos, its lack of motion, or its support mechanism.

Proper interpretation of the Bible depends on the type of literature that's being studied and the way words and phrases are used in different contexts throughout Scripture in their literary setting. "The term *literal* comes from the Latin *litera* meaning letter. To interpret the Bible literally is to interpret it as *literature*."[2]

Consider Daniel 4:11. The context describes a dream-vision that Nebuchadnezzar hAD In that dream he saw a tree "in the midst of the land, and its height was great" (4:10). Right away we should note that these images were seen in a dream as a series of visions. The fact that Daniel had to interpret the vision is an indication that the images in the dream represent other things (4:19–37). Nebuchadnezzar is the subject of the dream. He was like a tree in that he had "grown strong" and his "majesty had become great and reached to the sky" (4:22).

Some of the problems associated with interpreting the Bible literally happen because of translation issues. For example, many translations of Daniel 4:11 read this way: "And it was visible to the end of the whole **earth**." Critics of the Bible would say that this would be impossible if the biblical writers knew the earth was round. The Hebrew word *eretz* can be translated "earth" or "land," as in "the land of Israel" (Ezek. 12:19) and the "land of Shinar" (Dan. 1:2). The "earth of Israel" or the "earth of Shinar" would make no sense.

It would be difficult for a Golden-Rule literalist to deal with flat-earth and earth-centered language. "Common sense" observation did not lead scientists to conclude that the earth is a sphere. Even today, "common sense" observation shows the sun rises and sets around a stationary earth. The Bible is not attempting to teach a science lesson with these passages any more than newspapers are trying to be scientifically precise when they post when the sun will rise and set each day.

Map makers are no less scientific when they print flat maps with four corners. What should we think of the person who made a map of London shaped like a glove?[3]

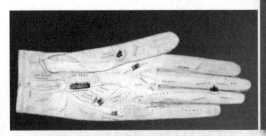

Figures of Speech

Metaphor: An implied (rather than actually stated) comparison between two things that are basically unalike (John 10:9).

Simile: Similar to a metaphor except the comparison is actually expressed using the words "like" or "as" (Job 41:24).

Metonymy: When one word or phrase is substituted for another with which it is closely associated (2 Cor. 3:15).

Synecdoche: When a part is used for the whole or the whole for a part, the special for the general or the general for the special (Jer. 25:29).

Personification: A writer speaks about (not to) a non-personal or non-living this as though it were a person (Deut. 32:1).

Apostrophe: Speech is directed to an imaginary person or abstract quality or idea (Isa. 54:1; Ezek. 37:4).

Hyperbole: Deliberate exaggeration for emphasis (Ps. 119:136).

Interrogation: Asks a question that has only one obvious answer (Jer. 32:27).

Irony: The use of words to convey a meaning that is the opposite of its literal meaning (2 Sam. 6:20; 1 Cor. 4:8).

Euphemism: Substituting a more agreeable or indirect expression for something unpleasant or seemingly offensive (Acts 7:60 ["fell asleep"]; Judges 3:24 ["covered his feet"]).

If this glove-shaped map was found buried under a mass of rubble three thousand years from now, would these future discoverers think that the person who made it believed that his world was shaped like a hand?

Let's look at another example. Some critics of the Bible claim that it teaches that the earth rests on "pillars" (1 Sam. 2:8; Job 9:6; 26:11). In these three cases, the word is found in a poetic literary structure. It's the **characteristics** of pillars that are important to the biblical writer.

Biblical authors were communicating in ways that people could understand. Like us, they were using literary devices to make a point. When we say someone is a "pillar in his community," do you suppose that people understand this to mean that he's holding up a building somewhere?

Notice this verse: "Now behold, I have made you today as a fortified city and **as a pillar of iron** and as **walls of bronze** against the whole land, to the kings of Judah, to its princes, to its priests and to the people of the land" (Jer. 1:18). Jeremiah has the **characteristics** of a fortified city, a pillar of iron, and walls of bronze.

In Psalm 144:12, the prayer is that the daughters of Israel will be "like corner pillars of a palace." In the same verse, the prayer is that Israel's sons will be "as grown-up plants." Once again, it's the attributes of pillars and plants that the author uses to make his points. The same is true when we read that Wisdom has built "her house . . . hewn out of seven pillars" (Prov. 9:1). Wisdom, because it's an abstract concept, needs concrete characteristics to make its principles concrete.

What's interesting is that the New Testament almost always uses "pillar" in a symbolic way. James, Peter, and John are "reputed to be pillars" in the church (Gal. 2:9). "The household of God, which is the church of the living

God," is "the **pillar** and support of the truth" (1 Tim. 3:15). We also read, "He who overcomes, Jesus "will **make him a pillar** in the temple" of God (Rev. 3:12). This final example will help with our understanding of how all of these examples relate to Bible prophecy:

> I saw another strong angel coming down out of heaven, clothed with a cloud; and the rainbow was upon his head, and his face was like the sun, and his feet like pillars of fire (Rev. 10:1).

In addition to the figurative use of "pillars," notice how heaven, a cloud, a rainbow, and the sun are being used in a symbolic way. Often times the use of stars, sun, moon, and clouds are used in prophetic sections of Scripture in a similar way. For example, in the Olivet Discourse we read, "But immediately after the tribulation of those days the sun will be darkened, and the moon will not give its light, and the stars will fall from heaven, and the powers of the heavens will be shaken" (Matt. 24:29). Is Jesus describing what will happen to the actual sun, moon, and stars, or is He borrowing the characteristics of these heavenly bodies from the way they are often used in the Old Testament?

The Bible often uses "sun," "moon," and "stars" to describe nations, in particular the nation of Israel. Consider

> "Then Joseph had a dream, and when he told it to his brothers, they hated him even more. He said to them, 'Please listen to this dream which I have had; for behold, we were binding sheaves in the field, and lo, my sheaf rose up and also stood erect; and behold, your sheaves gathered around and bowed down to my sheaf.' Then his brothers said to him, 'Are you actually going to reign over us? Or are you really going to rule over us?' So they hated him even more for his dreams and for his words. Now he had still another dream, and related it to his brothers, and said, 'Lo, I have had still another dream; **and behold, the sun and the moon and eleven stars were bowing down to me**.' He related it to his father and to his

brothers; and his father rebuked him and said to him, 'What is this dream that you have had? Shall I and your mother and your brothers actually come to bow ourselves down before you to the ground?'" (Gen. 37:5–10)

It's obvious that the sun, moon, and stars represent Jacob, Rachel, and Joseph's eleven brothers — the nation of Israel. In Revelation 12:1, we read about a "great sign" that "appeared in heaven: a woman clothed with the sun, and the moon under her feet, and on her head a crown of twelve stars." Most commentators agree that this image represents Israel. "In ancient cultures these astronomical symbols represented rulers. The **dream**, then symbolically anticipated the elevation of Joseph over the whole house of Jacob [Israel] (Joseph's **father**, the sun; his **mother**, the moon; his 11 **brothers**, the stars, v. 10)."[4]

"And behold, the sun and the moon and eleven stars were bowing down to me."

Tim LaHaye writes that the "woman clothed with the sun, and the moon under her feet," and having "on her head a crown of twelve stars" (Rev. 12:1) "is a reference to the nation of Israel."[5] He concludes that "they are symbolic of Israel. . . ."[6] So even someone like LaHaye who insists on a literal interpretation of the Bible acknowledges that not everything in the Bible is literal in the sense of just what is written.

Jesus borrows the sun, moon, and stars language from Isaiah 13:10 and 24:23 and Ezekiel 32:7 and Zephaniah 1:15 and applies them to the nation of Israel in His day. He knows that this type of language is used throughout the Old Testament to describe the judgment of nations, and He knew His audience would unuderstand the point He was making by using references to those pasages.

Consider this prophecy about the fall of Egypt by Old Testament Babylon:

> "'When I extinguish you [Egypt], I will cover the heavens, and **darken their stars**; I will **cover the sun with a cloud**, and the **moon shall not give its light**. All the shining lights in the heavens I will darken over you and will set darkness on your land,' declares the LORD" (Ezek. 32:7–8).

There's also this one that refers to the judgment of Edom, a long-ago vanquished enemy of Israel:

> And all the host of heaven will wear away,
> And the sky will be rolled up like a scroll;
> All their hosts will also wither away
> As a leaf withers from the vine,
> Or as *one* withers from the fig tree (Isa. 34:4).

John A. Martin's comments on Isaiah 13:10 are a helpful summary of how this language should be understood: "For the stars of heaven and their constellations will not flash forth their light; the sun will be dark when it rises and the moon will not shed its light."

The statements in 13:10 about the heavenly bodies (**stars … sun … moon**) no longer functioning may figuratively describe the total turnaround of the political structure of the Near East. The same would be true of **the heavens** trembling **and the earth** shaking (v. 13), figures of speech suggesting all-encompassing destruction.[7]

Jesus' disciples understood that Israel would come under a judgment similar to the judgment Babylon and other Old Testament nations experienced. *The language is nearly identical.* The interpretation should be equally nearly identical. Nothing actually happened to the sun, moon, and stars. They were symbols of national judgment. Jerusalem would be treated like the pagan nation of Babylon and other nations.

The events of history proved Jesus' words to be true. The Roman armies besieged Jerusalem in AD 70 and destroyed the temple so that not one stone was left upon another (Matt. 24:2).

Notes

1. Tim LaHaye, *No Fear of the Storm: Why Christians Will Escape All the Tribulation* (Sisters, OR: Multnomah, 1992), 240.

2. R. C. Sproul, *Knowing Scripture* (Downers Grove, IL: InterVarsity Press, 1977), 48.

3. Jayne Clark, "Map exhibits help navigate history and 'who we are,'" USA Today (November 2, 2007), 6D. It can be viewed online at www.usatoday.com/travel/destinations/2007-11-01-map-exhibits_N.htm

4. Allen P. Ross, "Genesis," *The Bible Knowledge Commentary: Old Testament*, eds. John F. Walvoord and Roy B. Zuck (Wheaton, IL Victor Books, 1985), 87.

5. Tim LaHaye, *Revelation Unveiled*, rev. ed. (Grand Rapids, MI: Zondervan, 1999), 198.

6. LaHaye, *Revelation Unveiled*, 198. Also see Tim LaHaye, ed. *Prophecy Study Bible* (Chattanooga, TN: AMG Publishers, 2000), 47, note on Genesis 37:6–11, and 1383, note on Revelation 12:1–5.

7. John A. Martin, "Isaiah," *The Bible Knowledge Commentary*, 1059.

A Beginner's Guide to Interpreting Bible Prophecy

PART 5

Making Sense of the Book of Revelation

Know the Old Testament

Revelation is a difficult book to understand. There's a dragon, a giant woman, scrolls, land and sea beasts, mysterious numbers, frightening marks, blasting trumpets, a thousand years, 200 million horse soldiers, stars falling from heaven that hit the earth, and so much more. What do they all mean?

Then there are all the things that are not in Revelation that we have been told can be found in Revelation. You won't find the words "antichrist," "rapture," or "millennium," any mention of a rebuilt temple, Jesus reigning on the earth for a 1000 years, a seven-year period of anything, or a treaty made with and then broken by "the antichrist."

Nothing is said about animals being sacrificed again for atonement (Ezek. 43:20; 45:25) or circumcision being reinstituted during the thousand years of Revelation 22. The number of the beast is not 6–6–6 but 666 (600+60+6).

In order to help in our understanding of the book of Revelation, we need to have

a good understanding of the rest of the Bible, especially the Old Testament. We also need to recognize the language of Revelation. While it was originally written in Greek and then translated into many other languages, its true language is in "symbols" or "signs," many of them based on concepts from the Old Testament. How do we know this? Revelation tells us.

Revelation or Revelations?

It's the book of *Revelation*, not the plural Revelation*s*: "The **Revelation** of Jesus Christ, which God gave Him to show to His bond-servants, the things which must **soon take place**; and He sent and communicated it by His angel to His bond-servant John, who testified to the word of God and to the testimony of Jesus Christ, even to all that he saw. Blessed is he who reads and those who hear the words of the prophecy, and heed the things which are written in it; for **the time is near**" (Rev. 1:1–3).

The word translated "communicated" in Revelation 1:1 is a Greek word best translated as "given for a sign." In order to understand this "sign language," we have to know how these symbols are used in other places in the Bible. The mind of the author of Revelation "was stored to a marvelous degree with the ideas, the language, and the imagery found in the Old Testament."

Without going into detail, consider how it would be easy to miss John's meaning if we did not realize that Balaam (2:14), Jezebel (2:20), a measuring rod (11:1), Egypt and Sodom (11:8), two witnesses, (11:3), Babylon (14:8; 16:19; 17:15; 18:2, 10), Gog and Magog (20:8) have

The Revelation that was given to John was to "signify" future events using images.

an Old Testament background filled with meaning. There is no way to understand how John is using these symbols until we know how they were used in their original Old Testament context.

It Matters when Revelation was Written

Knowing when Revelation was written can help those who read the prophecy to determine the period of time it was meant to be applied. We know that John tells us the things that were revealed to him were to take place "soon" or "shortly" (1:1) because "the time is near" (1:3).

In the final chapter of Revelation, John is told not to "seal up the words of the prophecy of this book, for the time is near" (22:10; cf. 1:3). Compare what was revealed to John to what was revealed to Daniel 600 hundred years before. Daniel was told to "seal up the book until" some particular end point in the future[1] (Dan. 12:4; cf. Dan 8:17; 12:9, 13). What is this a reference to? Most likely it refers to the "end" of the Old Covenant and the passing away of the shadows in animal sacrifices, an earthly sinful priesthood, and a stone temple. These shadows would be replaced with Jesus as the "lamb of God who takes away the sin of the world" (John 1:29), a priest "after the order of Melchizedek" (Heb. 7:17), and the temple of Jesus' own body (John 2:21).

This is why Peter could write, "the end of all things is at hand" (1 Peter 4:7; James 5:8) and the writer of Hebrews could open his letter with this declaration: "God, after He spoke long ago to the fathers in the prophets in many portions and

When Was Revelation Written?

The time texts describes events that were near to the time when John received the Revelation

> "The things that must soon take place" (1:1).

> "The time is near" (1:3).

> "I am coming quickly" (3:11).

> "The time is near" (22:10).

> "The things that are about to take place" (1:19).

> "That hour which is about to come upon the inhabited earth, to test those who dwell on the land" (3:10).

The Temple was destroyed in AD 70. It must have been still standing when John was told to measure it.

Continued

When Was Revelation Written? *continued*

"Then John was given a measuring rod like a staff and was told, 'Get up and measure the temple of God and the altar, and those who worship in it' " (11:1).

The number 666 corresponds to Nero Caesar

"Here is wisdom. Let him who has understanding calculate the number of the beast, for the number is that of a man; and his number is six hundred and sixty-six" (13:18).

John is writing during a time when the sixth Roman king (Nero Caesar) is alive.

"They are seven kings; five have fallen, one is, the other has not yet come" (17:10).

in many ways, *in these last days* has spoken to us in His Son, whom He appointed heir of all things, through whom also He made the world" (Heb. 1:1-2). Peter's "end of all things" that was near to the time of his writing refers to a "shadow" of what was promised "to come; but the substance belongs to Christ" (Col. 2:17) "so that all things which are written will be fulfilled" (Luke 21:22).

Peter wrote of his day that "the end of all things is at hand" (1 Peter 4:7)

When words like "near," "soon," and "shortly" are used in the Bible, they always refer to events that are about to take place. They never refer to distant events. The events in Revelation, therefore, describe prophetic events that were to take place near to the time John received the prophecy. Jesus' prediction of the destruction of the temple came to pass within a generation of Him giving the prophecy (Matt. 24:1-2, 34).

The End of the World or the End of Their World?

You might say, "But the language sounds like it's describing the end of the world as we know it." This is not the case when Revelation is read against the backdrop of the Old Testament and the way it describes local judgments using what sounds like end-of-the-world language.

Consider the prophet Micah's opening chapter:

> For behold, the Lord is coming forth from His place.
> He will come down and tread on the high places of
> the earth. The mountains will melt under Him and the
> valleys will be split, like wax before the fire, like water
> poured down a steep place (Micah 1:3–4).

This judgment was because of "the rebellion of Jacob" and "for the sins of the house of Israel" (1:5) in Micah's day. Even the use of "earth" does not make this a global judgment since the better translation is "land." Revelation is about God's righteous judgment against Israel that centered on the destruction of the temple that was still standing when John wrote down the revelation given to him.

Consider Isaiah 34:4 and the way it describes a local judgment:

> And all the host of heaven will wear away,
> And the sky will be rolled up like a scroll;
> All their hosts will also wither away
> As a leaf withers from the vine,
> Or as one withers from the fig tree.

Edom was the recipient of this end-of-the-world type judgment.

Study the book of Zephaniah 1 and notice how complete the judgments sound even though the judgments were "against Judah and against all the inhabitants of Jerusalem" (1:4):

> "I will completely remove all things
> From the face of the earth," declares the Lord.

"I will remove man and beast;
I will remove the birds of the sky
And the fish of the sea,
And the ruins along with the wicked;
And I will cut off man from the face of the earth,"
declares the Lord.

In Revelation 11:1, we learn that John was told, "Rise and measure the temple of God, and the altar, and those who worship in it." In the gospels, Jesus prophesied that the temple would be destroyed within a generation (Matt. 24:34) so that "not one stone here shall be left upon another, which will not be thrown down" (24:2). History records that Jesus' prophecy came to pass within a generation just as He stated. The temple in Jerusalem was destroyed by the Roman armies led by Titus in the year AD 70. If Revelation had been written after AD 70, there wouldn't have been a temple to measure. Since the New Testament doesn't say one thing about the temple being rebuilt, the temple John was told to measure must have been the one that was destroyed by the Romans. This makes perfect sense since John was told that the events in Revelation would happen "soon . . . for the time is near."

The destruction of Jesursalem in AD 70 by the Romans

Not everyone agrees with this argument. Some commentators argue for a date of composition near the end of the first century. But this makes little sense since this would contradict what Revelation says about events taking place "soon" because "the time is near." Then there is the problem of how

John could measure a temple that did not exist. There is no indication that it's a visionary temple since there are people still worshipping in it (11:1). It can't be a heavenly temple since "it has been given to the nations; and they will tread under foot the holy city for forty-two months" (11:2). There won't be any need for a physical temple in heaven or nations that would include unbelievers. Those who argue for a late date for Revelation's composition use questionable sources outside the Bible to make their case.[2]

The Whole World or John's World?

How do we explain Revelation 3:10 which reads, "Because you have kept the word of My perseverance, I also will keep you from the hour of testing, that hour which is about to come upon the whole world, to test those who dwell on the earth"? Read this way, the verse seems to be describing a worldwide event. Notice, however, that John says that the "hour of testing . . . is **about to come**." He is describing something that was on the horizon for him and his first readers.

You will find similar language in 1 John 2:18: "Children, it is **the last hour**; and just as you heard that antichrist is coming, **even now many antichrists have appeared**; from this we know that **it is the last hour**." John was describing events that were taking place in his day. How can these near events be reconciled with "the whole world" and "those who dwell on the earth"? Here's where Greek comes in again.

You will remember from Lesson 4 that the Greek word often translated "world" is not always **kosmos** (κοσμος), the word you would expect if the whole wide world was in view. But even when *kosmos* is used it can refer to an area less than worldwide (e.g., Rom. 1:8). Often times the word translated as "world" is **oikoumenē** (οικουμενη) which is better translated "inhabited earth," interpreted to mean the political boundaries of the then known world.

Then there is John's statement about testing "those who dwell upon the earth." Once again, knowing the Greek behind the translation helps. The Greek word for "earth" is best translated as "land." John seems to be describing prophetic events that were "about to happen" to those who first read Revelation.

Stars or Meteorites?

Let's apply the principles we've learned so far by looking at three examples from Revelation. We read in Revelation 8:10 that "a great star fell from heaven, burning like a torch, and it fell on a third of the rivers." If one star hits the earth, the earth would be vaporized in an instant. In fact, if a star gets even close to the earth, the earth is going to burn up before it hits. Notice Revelation 8:12: "Then the fourth angel sounded, and a third of the sun and a third of the moon and a third of the stars were smitten, so that a third of them might be darkened and the day might not shine for a third of it, and the night in the same way."

How can a "third of the sun" be smitten without catastrophic results on the whole earth and not just a third of it? All of this language is drawn from the Old Testament and only has meaning as it is interpreted in light of its Old Testament context — the judgment and destruction of nations (Isa. 14:12; Jer. 9:12–16; Ezek. 5:2, 12), in particular, the nation of Israel in the first century (Matt. 24:1–34).

Some claim that the "stars" are actually meteorites. If this is the case, then there is a problem with Revelation 12:4 where a "great red dragon" uses his "tail" to sweep a "third of the stars of heaven" to throw "them to the earth." Such a barrage would destroy the earth, making it uninhabitable for man and beast for millennia. And yet, we are to believe that the armies of the entire world are going to pick a fight with Israel (Rev. 16:13–16) after a third of the earth's population has been wiped out.

It's in Revelation 9:15 that the four angels "kill a third of mankind." If this judgment takes place in the land of Israel, then the use of "mankind" (lit., *men*) is a reference to those living in Israel during the time of the siege. Josephus, a Jewish historian for the Romans, records that more than a million Jews were killed during the war. This number is probably more than a third of the population, but we know that there were judgments to come (Rev. 16) before the final Roman onslaught against the temple. Eventually the total number killed came to two-thirds of the population (Zech. 13:8), the million mentioned by Josephus.

Armageddon: Past or Future?

Notice something important about the so-called "Battle of Armageddon" (16:16). John writes that the "kings of the whole world" will gather "together for the war of the great day of God, the Almighty" (16:14). Many see this as a world-wide conflagration because of the use of "whole world." But it's not. The Greek word for "world" is *oikoumenē* (not *kosmos*), the same word used in Matthew 24:14, Luke 2:1, and Revelation 3:10, is a reference to the then-known world. The battle is waged by the world empire of the day—Rome—made up of many nations. The phrase is used in a similar way in the Old Testament.[3]

Chinese Soldiers or a Demonic Army?

What of the 200 million troops on horseback (Rev. 9:16)? There aren't 200 million horses in the entire world today. At most there are 65 million, and this includes all types if equine. Even many who interpret Revelation as applying to a yet future time see this imagery as symbolic. Why would these nations mount such a vast army after a third of the earth's population (not to mention hours) has just been wiped out by plagues and falling stars to the earth? It doesn't make any sense. The world would be in such chaos that the last thing on anyone's mind would be to round up 200 million horses, soldiers, weapons, saddles, and enough food and water so they could make a nearly impossible trek from China (16:12) to Israel. Do we not remember how the world went on hold after 9–11? It seems obvious from Revelation 9:17 that this is a symbolic army, a demon-inspired army bent on destruction (9:1–11). The comments by Ralph E. Bass, Jr., are helpful:

[This] is a number designed to terrorize. And indeed, that is its achieved result. As Carrington says, ". . . it is the empire of hell." There never has been such an army and apparently never will be one. . . . But the number appears to have another meaning than the number of Roman soldiers from that area; it appears to suggest the number of demons that were released on Israel and Jerusalem. Remember the story of the demon possessed man from Garasenes (Luke 8:30)? He was possessed by a legion of demons. A legion was from 5,000 to 6,000 men, and all this in but one man! At 6,000 demons per person, it would only require a little over 33,000 inhabitants of Judah to justify these numbers.[4]

Summary

Being able to interpret the Bible requires knowledge of the Bible. This is especially true with the subject of prophecy. The Bible is the best interpreter of itself. Remember to keep the primary audience in mind, pay attention to time texts, compare Scripture with Scripture, and literal refers to the type of literature that's being used.

Notes

1. The Hebrew word *qets* refers to events "*at the end of* a period time." Essentially, the end of what?

2. For a study of this subject, see Kenneth L. Gentry, Jr., *Before Jerusalem Fell: Dating the Book of Revelation* (Powder Springs, GA: American Vision, 1998); Kenneth L. Gentry, Jr., *The Beast of Revelation* (Powder Springs, GA: American Vision, 2002); Gary DeMar and Francis X. Gumerlock, *The Early Church and the End of the World* (Powder Springs, GA: American Vision, 2006).

3. See Gary DeMar, *Why the End of the World is Not in Your Future: Identifying the Gog-Magog Alliance* (Powder Springs, GA: American Vision, 2008).

4. Ralph E. Bass, *Back to the Future: A Study in the Book of Revelation* (Greenville, SC: Living Hope Press, 2004), 241.

Gary DeMar, *Is Jesus Coming Soon?*

Gary DeMar, *Last Days Madness.*

Gary DeMar, *Why the End of the World is Not in Your Future.*

Gary DeMar, *Left Behind: Separating Fact from Fiction.*

Gary DeMar, *10 Popular Prophecy Myths Exposed and Answered.*

Gary DeMar, *Identifying the Real Last Days Scoffers.*

Gary DeMar, *Prophecy Wars: The Biblical Battle Over the End Times.*

Gary DeMar and Francis X. Gumerlock,
The Early Church and the End of the World.

Francis X. Gumerlock, *Revelation and the First Century.*

Francis X. Gumerlock, *The Day and the Hour:*
Christianity's Perennial Fascination with Predicting the End of the World.

Kenneth L. Gentry, Jr., *Before Jerusalem Fell: Dating the Book of Revelation.*

Kenneth L. Gentry, Jr., *The Book of Revelation Made Easy.*

Kenneth L. Gentry, Jr. and Thomas Ice, *The Great Tribulation:*
Past or Future?: Two Evangelicals Debate the Question.

John L. Bray, *Matthew 24 Fulfilled.*

Steve Gregg, *Revelation: Four Views*
(A Parallel Commentary).

David Chilton, *The Days of Vengeance:*
An Exposition of the Book of Revelation

David Chilton, *Paradise Restored: A Biblical Theology of Dominion.*

David Chilton, *The Great Tribulation.*

Dwight Wilson, *Armageddon Now! The Premillenarian Response to*
Russia and Israel Since 1917.